John Ballinger

The Cardiff free libraries

John Ballinger

The Cardiff free libraries

ISBN/EAN: 9783742899460

Manufactured in Europe, USA, Canada, Australia, Japa

Cover: Foto ©Thomas Meinert / pixelio.de

Manufactured and distributed by brebook publishing software
(www.brebook.com)

John Ballinger

The Cardiff free libraries

LIST OF ILLUSTRATIONS.

View of Library Building, Trinity Street. Facing title.

Portrait of the late Peter Price, J.P. Facing page 1.

Portrait of the late Charles Thompson, J.P. Facing page 5.

Facsimile from MS. called " Hanesyn Hên." Page 33.

Facsimile from MS. called " Trefydd Marchnad Cymry." Page 34.

Facsimiles of Autographs of Welsh Literary men, from original letters in the library collection. Pages 35—7.

Titlepages of—

    H. Lloyd's " Commentarioli Britannicæ," 1572. Page 38.

        " Breviary of Britain," 1573. Page 39.

        " Historie of Cambria," 1584. Page 40.

    " A Briefe and Necessarie Catechisme, set forth by Richard Jones, Schoole-master in Cardiff." (1600). Page 41.

    " The Leaves of the Tree of Life," by Edmund Jones, Carmarthen, 1745. Page 42.

PETER PRICE, J.P.

 HE honour of first suggesting that Cardiff should adopt the Public Libraries Act belongs to the late Mr. Peter Price, whose many years of patient hard work will be remembered as long as the Library records endure.

In the year 1858 Mr. Price wrote letters to the Cardiff newspapers advocating the adoption of the Act and the establishment of a Library. For two years nothing definite was done, although the letters had borne fruit by enlisting the services of Mr. George Smart, a member of the Town Council, who worked zealously with Mr. Price.

It was in 1860 that the first practical step was taken towards inducing the ratepayers to establish a Library. On the 24th October in that year a public meeting of ratepayers was held in the British School-room, Millicent Street, to consider the advisability of adopting the Act. Mr. George Smart was voted to the chair. The attendance was very meagre, only about 35 ratepayers being present. An address was made by the Chairman, followed by Mr. Charles Thompson, who made an earnest speech in favour of the proposed library. The meeting was very apathetic, there was no touch of enthusiasm, although a resolution in favour of the Library was carried with but five dissentients.

On the following Tuesday, October 30th, a meeting of burgesses was held at the Town Hall to decide whether the Libraries Act should be put into force. At the appointed hour for the commencement of the business (7 o'clock) not more than nine burgesses were present; and it was suggested that as the pending municipal election appeared to absorb all the interest for the moment an adjournment should take place, "but this was over-ruled by the majority, and "it was determined to wait a bit. Twenty minutes "passed in silence, except by the representatives of "the press, who passed their time pleasantly by "cracking jokes. At length some half-dozen bur-"gesses and inhabitants made their appearance, "among whom were Mr. Langley and Mr. Cory, "Town Councillors. The spirit of the meeting began "to cheer up, and it was anticipated that there would "be a 'jolly bit of fun,' as some well-known antagon-"ists on public occasions had put in an appearance." A good number of people subsequently turned up, including the Mayor (Mr. Wm. Alexander) and the Town Clerk. So eager were the opponents of educational progress that one of them at once proposed that the Act be not adopted, and this being seconded, the proposal to adopt the Act was put forward as an amendment by the Rev. N. Thomas and seconded by Mr. George Smart.

The discussion was animated and prolonged. The economical ratepayer who saw ruin ahead was well to

CHARLES THOMPSON, J.P.

the front; it was suggested that only a few faddists wished to have a Library, and that if it were established it would not be used and would have to be closed again. One haughty opponent objected to be taxed for a Library, but he would be willing to subscribe his "mite to open a Free Library for the *lower classes.*" He was equal to his word, his name appears in the voluntary library subscription list for £5 5s.

The adoption of the Act was advocated by Mr. Charles Thompson, Mr. W. (? Wyndham) Lewis, Mr. Richard Cory (Senr.), Mr. Smart, Mr. Peter Price, and others. On being put to the vote, 31 voted for the adoption of the Act, and 32 against. A subscription list was at once started for providing a voluntary Free Library, the Mayor of Cardiff (the late Alderman William Alexander) starting the list with ten guineas. About £60 was subscribed in the room, and the amount altogether ultimately reached £189 17s. 9d.

The scheme for a voluntary library and reading room was pushed forward with vigour. A meeting of subscribers was held a fortnight after the public meeting, and a Committee was appointed to manage the Institution, Mr. Alexander being appointed Treasurer, and Mr. Peter Price Honorary Secretary. Colonel Stuart, M.P. for Cardiff, was made President, and a number of gentlemen were nominated as Patrons and Vice-Presidents. Some difficulty was experienced in finding suitable premises; eventually a room at the St. Mary Street end of the Royal Arcade was constructed by Messrs. James and Price, the rent of opened on the 15th June, 1861. The attendance at this reading room was so large that in a few months the opponents of the library movement were converted, and at a public meeting convened by the Mayor, and held at the Town Hall on the 22nd September, 1862, a large number of ratepayers attended, and the Act was carried with only one dissentient. The Mayor of Cardiff (Alderman C. W. David) who presided, cordially supported the proposal to establish a library, and the formal motion to adopt the Act was proposed by Mr. Charles Thompson and seconded by Dr. Vachell.

The Committee of the voluntary library at once agreed to hand over the reading room and the property acquired to the Committee to be appointed by the Corporation, and on the 9th of November, 1862, the Corporation voted a sum of £450—being the equivalent of a penny rate—to defray the expenses for one year, and appointed a Committee to carry out the Act.

A report published in July, 1862, by the Committee of the voluntary library states that the number of visits to the Reading Room for the year was 95,625; the number of books in the library was 400, all of them presented, and the number of loans of books was 4,343 for ten months. The salary of the Librarian was £20 per annum, out of which he had to pay a boy to

THE MUSEUM AND SCHOOLS.

On the 27th October, 1862, the Corporation appointed a Committee to carry out the Libraries Act in the Borough. It will be interesting, after so many years, to recall the names of the first members elected on the Committee. Here is the list :—

The Mayor (Alderman C. W. David).
He was Mayor five times.
C. R. Vachell,. M.D.   (Born 1813 ; died 26th May, 1865).
E. Whiffen (Mayor of Cardiff 1869-70).
Wm. Alexander (Hon. Treasurer, Alderman and J.P., Mayor of Cardiff 1859-60).
William Nell.
Daniel Jones (Alderman, J.P., Mayor of Cardiff 1874-5-6).
R. H. Mitchel.
H. Bowen (Alderman, J.P., Mayor of Cardiff 1872-3).
W. T. Edwards, M.D.
M. Grover.
H. Bird.
E. P. Richards (declined to act).
Charles Thompson (Deputy-Chairman.   Died June 1st, 1889).
E. S. Hill (now Sir Edward S. Hill, K.C.B., M.P. He declined to act, but has always taken an interest in the Library).
John Batchelor (died 1883.   Mayor 1853-4).

Wm. Vachell (born 1827. Mayor of Cardiff 1873-4).

J. Tomlinson.

S. P. Kernick.

Jonas Watson.

Henry Heard.

D. L. Thomas.

Morris Phillips.

Peter Price (Hon. Secretary, afterwards Chairman;
    a member of the Corporation and a J.P.; died
    1892).

E. Mason.

The Committee appointed the Mayor for the time
being as Chairman, and Mr. Charles Thompson
Deputy-Chairman. Mr. Alexander was Treasurer,
and Mr. Peter Price Hon. Secretary.

One of the first topics discussed by the Committee
was the propriety of opening a branch reading-room,
and the question of convenient premises was also gone
into at the first meeting. It is worthy of note that the
site for a new building which found most favour with
the Committee was one in the Hayes, and that,
although this was abandoned at the time, yet, after
years of storm and stress, during which the "battle
of the sites" raged continuously, the Library has found
its permanent home in the district first proposed.

The Newsroom was carried on for a short time
after the adoption of the Act in the premises at the
end of the Royal Arcade. Eventually the Committee
entered into an agreement for a tenancy of the building
belonging to the Young Men's Christian Association
in St. Mary Street, at a rental of £100 per annum,
from the 1st January, 1864.

The Lending Library was opened to the public about October 13th, 1863, with a total stock of 1,076 volumes. The Reference Library at the same date is reported as containing 49 volumes. An interesting detail is that this modest stock of books comprised a copy of the Bible in Dr. Moon's embossed type for the use of the blind. I am afraid from the evidence before me, that the 49 volumes which formed the nucleus of a reference library were a few blue books, and some lumber which could not possibly be offered to lending library readers.

The first year's work in the Lending Library gave a total issue of 7,717 volumes, which increased during the next year to 12,187 volumes. The early years of the Lending Library were very chequered, and although some progress was made each year it was very slight. In 1873, ten years after the first opening of the Lending Library, the total stock was 7,296, and the number of volumes lent 22,711. Although a few books had been acquired and set aside from time to time for a Reference Library, there is no record that any use was made of them. It was not until 20 years after the adoption of the Act that the reference department was formally recognised, the number of volumes issued for reference in 1883-4 being recorded as 6,291, the lending library figures for the same year being 64,222.

In all the early reports of the Committee the News-room appears to have the first place, and the major part of the money was expended in this direction. The use made of this department was considerable—an accurate report of the numbers was kept, a boy being employed to record each person who entered the reading room. In 1861-2, the number of visitors to the voluntary reading room was 96,000, the first year after the adoption of the Act the number rose to 145,000, and two years later it was 222,500.

In the circular issued by the original promoters the object is stated to be "the establishment of a Refer-"ence and Circulating Library and Reading-Room "... as well as a room for the reception of "Antiquities, Curiosities, Botanical and Geological "specimens, and objects in Natural History."

A Museum was clearly part of the scheme as put forward by the promoters, but the first step towards the collection of objects to form a Museum was deferred for two or three years. In December, 1863, a Sub-Committee was appointed to manage and arrange the Museum, and a month later a sum of £50 was voted for the purchase of cases, and the "back room on the top storey" of the St. Mary Street building was appropriated for the Museum. In this room was stored the objects contributed from time to time. The progress made was slow, and the "back room on the top storey" sufficed as a store for some years.

In June, 1867, Mr. Philip Stewart Robinson, better known in these days as "Phil Robinson," the author of several popular works on natural history, was appointed librarian, and his appointment had an important influence on the future of the Museum. An enthusiastic naturalist, and a genial and cultured gentleman, he quickly made his way into the good graces of the local people interested in natural science, and a Society for the study of natural history and the collection of objects for the local Museum was soon

formed, mainly through the exertions of Mr. Robinson.
To this Society, "The Cardiff Naturalists' Society,"
which is still flourishing, the care of the infant
Museum was committed, through its aid the scheme was
gradually realised, and it is to the fostering care
of the members of the Society that the town owes
many of the collections now in the Museum. The
public were admitted to view the specimens on two
evenings weekly from January, 1872, by which time
some valuable gifts of show-cases, geological specimens, birds, and sculpture had been received, and the
whole had been put into a fit state for exhibition. A
number of rooms had been thrown into one large one,
and the geological collection had been arranged and
named by Mr. Robert Etheridge, F.R.S.

While the Museum part of the scheme was still
unrealized, the Committee undertook the organization
of Science and Art Classes. In the report issued in
November, 1865, the name of the Institution appears
for the first time as the "Cardiff Free Library, Museum
and Schools of Science and Art," a name under which
it was to continue for more than a quarter of a century.
This report says "A distinguishing feature of the past
year has been the addition of Science and Art Schools
to the Institution. A public meeting of the ratepayers
and others, presided over by the Mayor, passed a
resolution recommending their adoption, on the occasion
of the visit of Mr Buckmaster, of the Science and Art
Department, to this town. The Schools which were
commenced in accordance with this recommendation
have been in successful operation for nine months, and
bid fair to attain permanent success."

The anticipations of the Committee were fully realised with regard to the Schools. Under the guiding hand of an able and energetic Head Master, Mr. James Bush, B.Sc. (happily, still with us), the Schools so modestly began were destined to play a very important part in the educational life of Cardiff, and I firmly believe that the brilliant careers of many of the students did a great deal to pave the way for the magnificent educational developments which have been carried out in Cardiff during recent years.

With a Library and its appurtenances, a Museum, and Schools of Science and Art, all to be supported from a grant of £450, of which £100 was deducted for rent, the Committee of the young Institution had not much cash to spare for the purchase of books for the Library, and as no funds were forthcoming from other quarters the collection of books did not make much progress.

There was still a certain amount of prejudice against the Institution existing in some minds; and although many members of the Corporation were warm supporters, yet there was a niggardly spirit displayed in voting money. Instead of giving the Library Committee the proceeds of a penny rate, the Corporation voted a round sum annually, and I have good reason for saying that the amount voted was always well *under* the amount produced by a penny rate. This continued for about fifteen years, and was the subject of some very keen fighting until about 1877, when a more liberal policy was adopted; but it is only quite recently that the Corporation has voted for the year the full proceeds of a penny rate as represented by the valuation of the year in which it is paid—an important detail in Cardiff, where the assessments increase very rapidly.

THE BUILDING SCHEMES AND THE RESULT.

It would probably be hard to find an Institution which has been the subject of so many building schemes as the Cardiff Free Library. From the year 1862, almost to the present time, Committee after Committee has been busy with the question of suitable buildings and available sites.

The first proposal was made in 1862, to acquire what was known as the Waterloo site in the Hayes, where the building used as a Salvation Army Barracks, and formerly called the Stuart Hall, now stands. This was abandoned in favour of a site on the Bulwarks in St. Mary Street, where the Philharmonic Hall and Restaurant now are. Mr. Waring prepared plans and drawings for a building on this site to be erected at a cost of £3,000, but the project was abandoned in favour of the Young Men's Christian Association building, also in St. Mary Street, which was leased for ten years. Before the term expired the Science and Art Classes were removed to rooms at the east end of the Royal Arcade in order to give extra space to the Museum.

During the years 1872-1880, some scheme for a new building or the adaptation of a building was constantly before the public. The sites proposed amongst others were :—

The present Theatre Royal site.

Westgate Street—site of new Post Office.

Site where Park Hotel and Park Hall
now stand.

The Old Infirmary, now University
College.

The Market site, St. Mary Street entrance
to Market.

The Custom House.

Teigil Buildings, St. Mary Street, now
entrance to Wyndham Arcade.

The site of the present Municipal Offices
between the Town Hall and old
Post Office.

Plans were prepared for several of these schemes,
and attempts were made to enlist public support.
Lord Bute offered the Westgate Street site and a
handsome contribution to the building fund, but un-
fortunately the offer was not accepted.

The Zion Chapel site ultimately chosen was acquired under a local improvement Act, and under the
powers conferred by the Public Libraries Act the Corporation set aside a portion of the land so purchased
for the purposes of the Libraries Act, and proceeded to
erect a building for the Library, Museum, and Science
and Art Schools. This building is the older wing of
the buildings now brought to completion. It was
opened to the public in May, 1882, with considerable
eclat, by Mr. Alfred Thomas (now M.P. for East
Glamorgan), the Mayor of Cardiff for that year. The
total cost was about £11,000, exclusive of decorations
contributed from various sources.

The interest taken in the building by the public
found expression in the extensive support accorded

to a Fine Art and Industrial Exhibition, inaugurated with a view to raising funds for the furnishing and equipment of the building, from which a surplus fund amounting to £1,300 resulted. This money was expended on decorations and the purchase of pictures and china for the Museum, books for the Library, and examples and apparatus for the Schools of Science and Art. An important outcome of the Exhibition was the presentation by Sir E. J. Reed (M.P. for the Borough 1880-1895), of the magnificent painting " Noon on the Surrey Hills," by Vicat Cole. This fine gift was followed by an offer from Mr. William Menelaus, the General Manager of the Dowlais Iron Works, to give from his collection paintings to the value of £10,000. This offer was most cordially accepted by the Corporation, and the paintings were selected by the well-known expert, Mr. William Agnew. Various gifts of pictures and works of art followed, and, with some sculpture given in earlier years, formed the nucleus of an Art Gallery.

The Library also received a gift of about 2,000 volumes, being a portion of the valuable library of His Honour Judge Falconer, which he bequeathed between three towns, Newport, Cardiff, and Swansea. Mr. Falconer had always taken a warm interest in the progress of these three libraries.

FROM ADVERSITY TO PROSPERITY.

ADOPTION OF THE
TECHNICAL INSTRUCTION ACT.

When the new building was completed and occupied the amount paid to the Libraries Committee on account of the rate was £1,088, a sum of £422 being deducted for interest and redemption of loan—the total rate therefore was £1,510. Out of this sum of £1,088 the Committee had to support the three institutions— Library, Museum, and Schools. The whole amount was practically absorbed in expenses of administration, and very little progress was made in the collection of a library. The amount available each year for binding was so limited that the books wore a neglected look, and the books were circulated long after they ought in decency to have been withdrawn. Files of newspapers and volumes of magazines were piled away in store-rooms unbound. The arrears of bookbinding were so heavy that even yet they have not been completely overtaken.

To illustrate in a practical way the backward condition of the Library when it was removed to the new building, I have made a calculation of the amounts expended on books and bookbinding during periods of ten years: the result is as follows:—

		Books.			Bookbinding.				Total.		
		£	s.	d.	£	s.	d.		£	s.	d.
1863-1872	...	938	18	10	... 267	0	1	...	1,205	18	11
1873-1882	...	1,227	7	0	... 536	8	7	...	1,763	15	7
1883-1892	...	3,980	13	7	... 1,264	13	5	...	5,245	7	0
1892-3	...	653	4	0	... 274	11	5	...	927	15	5
1893-4	...	610	10	6	... 151	16	0	...	762	6	6
Total	...	£7,410	13	11	...£2,494	9	6	...£9,905	3	5	

The removal took place at the end of the second period of ten years. For the first two years of the third period, the funds of the Institution were in a pitiful state, and practically no additions were made to the stock, which was then about 15,000 volumes; but in 1885, a new assessment of the property in the Borough raised the penny rate to an amount which enabled the Committee to expend £494 8s. 7d. on books and binding in that year, and from 1885 what I call the period of prosperity begins. The good use made of the funds greatly increased the popularity of the Library with the townspeople; and when the Technical Instruction Act was passed, it was immediately adopted without opposition, Cardiff being one of the first, if not the first, town to adopt the Act. By transferring the cost of maintaining the Science and Art Schools to a rate levied under the Technical Instruction Act, the Corporation not only relieved the Library funds, but also provided a scheme of technical instruction which was commensurate with the increasing needs of the town. The old Science and Art Schools filled an important place in local education, and the new Technical School, carried on in conjunction with the University College, has amplified and improved the facilities for this branch of education. The schools were transferred to the new authority on the 6th September, 1890. Classes were continued in the Library building for one year, after which the rooms used by the schools were appropriated for the storage of books.

Reference has already been made to the bequest of 2,000 volumes made by Judge Falconer. Other gifts of value have been made in the last twelve years by the Marquess of Bute, Colonel Page, the Trustees of the British Museum, and by Mr. Herbert M. Thompson, M.A. The last-named gentleman is the most liberal helper the Library has had. He purchased and presented to the Library a complete set of the Reports of the "Challenger" expedition, and sets of the proceedings and transactions of the Royal Society, the Linnean Society, the Ray Society, and the Zoological Society. Mr. Thompson has also been a liberal donor of books to the Canton Branch.

The Committee for many years endeavoured to form a library of books in Welsh and relating to Wales, but with modest results, until in 1891 it was decided to purchase the collection made by the Rees family of Llandovery, the well-known printers of the "Liber Landavensis," the "Mabinogion," and other works relating to Wales. This collection contained about 7,000 volumes of printed books, 100 volumes of MS., and a large number of local maps and prints. A portion of the cost was defrayed by subscription.

Additions have been made to this collection from various sources, and the Library now possesses a collection of Welsh books and books on Wales of which we are very proud.

EXTENSION OF THE BUILDINGS.

ADOPTION OF THE MUSEUMS ACT.

The improved financial position of the Institution was very quickly appreciated by the public, and the building opened in 1882 was three years later quite unequal to the requirements of the town—the rooms were too small, the book storage too limited, and in some parts of the building the light was not good. To Mr. John Gunn belongs the honour of being the first to foresee what was necessary, and it was through his action that the Corporation, of which he was then a member, reserved the piece of ground adjoining for an extension of the building. This piece of ground was then covered with small tenements, stables, and workshops, and the nature of the buildings was a constant source of danger to the Library.

The first intention of the Committee was to erect buildings providing additional accommodation for the Library, the Museum, and the Science and Art Schools. But so rapidly do events move in Cardiff, that before the scheme was finally approved the adoption of the Technical Instruction Act relieved the Committee from the need to provide for the Schools, making it possible to devote much more and better space to the Library and Museum.

A new scheme was prepared, and was on the point of being carried out, when the passing of the Museums and Gymnasiums Act again induced the authorities to pause. The Corporation, acting on the recommendation of the Free Libraries Committee, decided to put the new Act in force so far as it relates to the Museum, and thereby relieve the Library rate from this charge. The Museum was transferred to a new authority appointed under the Museums Act, from the 1st March, 1893. It was quickly agreed that in the interests of the Museum and of the Library it would be desirable to erect a building for the Museum on another site.

The way was now clear for the extension of the Library, and work was begun in the autumn of 1893.

The cost of the extension is about £15,000, exclusive of furnishing ; neither does this sum include the cost of setting back the east front of the old building for the widening of Working Street. By this latter work the street will be widened over 15 feet, a most desirable improvement, the expense of which will be charged to Public Works.

The chief aim of the Committee has been to provide in the new building large and well-lighted Reading Rooms for newspapers and magazines, and for the Reference Library, and to utilise the old wing for the Lending Library, and for book storage. A new entrance, wide and lofty, will entirely supersede the two entrances formerly in use. It was felt to be desirable to have all persons entering and leaving the building under control, and a Porter's lodge has been placed in the new entrance for this purpose.

Immediately to the right after entering is the News and Magazine Room, an arrangement which diverts a considerable proportion of the visitors from the corridor immediately they enter the building. A staircase to the left leads to the Reference Library. At the end of the main corridor is the Ladies' Reading Room, and a short passage leads to the borrowers' hall of the Lending Library, which takes all the ground floor of the old building.

In the main corridor a drinking fountain has been placed for public use, and a similar fountain has been provided in the Reference Library for the readers.

The whole building is warmed with hot water on the low pressure system. It is lighted with the electric light, incandescent lamps are used, and the power is supplied from the Corporation works. The tables in the Reading Rooms are lighted by means of standards fixed to the floor, a much more satisfactory method than hanging lamps from the ceiling.

The News and Magazine Room contains about 450 superficial yards of floor space, and provides comfortably for 280 persons reading at one time. The reading stands are arranged around the walls of the room, and the tables at which readers will be seated occupy the centre floor space. By this means the Reading Room Attendant has full control of the readers. All periodicals regularly supplied are provided with a fixed location, the newspapers on the reading stands, and other periodicals by attaching the reading cases to a string fastened underneath the table. By allowing a yard of cord to each periodical a reader is enabled to lift it from the table and read it in almost any position. An enamelled plate giving the title of each newspaper and periodical is placed above or in front of its location, and at the tables a chair is allotted to each periodical. The newspapers and periodicals are arranged in alphabetical order, and a periodical rack and a spare table provides for a few publications to which places cannot be allotted. Tables are also provided for writing. The time tables are placed on a stand-up desk on one side of the room near the entrance, and the local directories will be placed on the same desk, and screwed down. By these means we have avoided the untidiness and confusion which is such a drawback to reading rooms; readers can see at a glance what periodicals are in use, and no person is able to appropriate more than one at a time. The reading desks are made of pitch pine, and the tables of polished birch.

The Ladies' Room provides for 43 readers, and is arranged on exactly the same lines as the Newsroom. The furniture is polished birch, and the floor is covered with cork carpet.

The Reference Library provides for 143 readers, special desks being provided for directories, newspaper files, and other large volumes. Provision has also been made for special students. On a counter running across the room the Card Catalogue of the Reference Library will be arranged in a cabinet of 24 drawers. In a bookcase with plate glass front the most recent additions to the Reference Library will be displayed. The books are stored in presses behind the counter, and the presses are continued in one series throughout the first floor of the old and new buildings. The immediate storage capacity for the Reference Library is about 60,000 volumes. On the removal of the Museum two or three years hence the storage space will be increased to an almost unlimited extent, and it will be possible to provide for at least 250,000 volumes. I hope the need for this will some day be realised. A special room has been set aside for the Welsh collection which forms such an important feature of the Library.

The floor of the Reference Library is covered with cork carpet, and the furniture is made of teak, except the chairs, which are made of polished beech.

The Lending Library is provided for on the ground floor of the old building. A large central borrowers' hall, fitted with catalogue tables, seats, and other conveniences gives ample space for 150 borrowers. The indicators are arranged on two sides of the hall, and the books are stored in alcoves immediately behind the indicators, and an open counter at one end of the hall will enable borrowers to exchange their books, and make inquiries in comfort. Book storage is provided for about 50,000 volumes in this department, which can be increased if required. All the chairs in the building are fitted with Cotton's indiarubber pads, which considerably reduces the amount of noise made in moving them about.

The cost of furnishing, about £2,000, has been defrayed from a special fund accumulated for the purpose by setting aside a sum annually from the penny rate during the last few years.

Speaking-tubes connect the various departments with one another, and with the librarian, who is provided with a handsome room on the first floor.

The Newsroom, Reference Library, and Ladies' Room, give adequate accommodation for 466 readers at one time. The old building was uncomfortably crowded with 150 readers.

THE BRANCHES.

The question of Branch Reading Rooms was raised immediately after the adoption of the Libraries Act in 1862, and continued to re-appear at intervals until the Committee took steps to establish the Branches in 1889. It formed the topic for many a stirring election-eering speech, and was a certain win for candidates for municipal honours.

The financial burden involved was, however, more than the Committee felt justified in undertaking, so long as the Central Library remained in an im-poverished state. The desirability of Branches was never contested; the reason for delay in their establish-ment was financial.

The hand of the Committee was, however, forced at length, and a sum of £30 each was offered towards the cost of a Branch in each of the five outlying districts for one year. This sum was utterly inadequate for the purpose, but thanks to the enthusiasm of a number of willing workers the offer of the Committee was supplemented by outside help, and in the course of a couple of years five branch reading rooms were in operation. The Committee increased the amounts granted to each district as the funds at its disposal allowed, and eventually in 1893 took over the entire cost and the management.

The five branch reading rooms taken over are still in operation, together with a sixth which has been erected by the Committee on a site given by Lord Tredegar at Splotlands. The last named is so far the only branch which is equal to the requirements of the district it serves. The branch at Canton is fairly adequate, but it consists of two rooms on separate floors, and is therefore very difficult of supervision. The reading room at Grangetown is much too small, while the other three at Cathays, Roath, and the Docks are only makeshifts.

Efforts are being made to secure sites and erect buildings in each of these districts.

Each of the Branches is well supplied with newspapers and periodicals, and at each there is a stock of books, varying from 300 to 1,500 volumes, to be read on the premises. In four of the Branches the books are in an open book case, and readers are allowed access to them without any supervision beyond that of the reading room attendant. The plan has worked fairly well, and is very popular, but it has met with some abuse from systematic book thieves, but not more than was anticipated when the plan was projected.

At the Canton Branch the books were given by three gentlemen, Mr. Herbert M. Thompson, Mr. Alexander Thompson, and Mr. Alderman Sanders, with the understanding that the open access was to be tried. The books were particularly well selected. It is here perhaps that the scheme has met with most success, and most abuse. The books at Grangetown have been bought with moneys given from time to time by Mr. Councillor Brain, and the books at Roath and the Docks have all been given by various donors.

The public fully appreciate these district Reading Rooms, they are always well attended, and the conduct of the readers is good.

The completion of the Central Library will enable the Committee to give more attention to the improvement of the Branches.

THE PRESENT AND THE FUTURE.

The Central Library at the present time consists of about 55,000 volumes, of which about 30,000 volumes are in the Reference department, and the balance in the Lending department.

The use made by the public during the last complete year, 1893-94, was :—Lending Library 164,781 volumes lent, Reference Library 31,605. Both departments have shown large increases for the current year, and when the new buildings are in full operation a rapid development is expected.

The number of visitors to the Central Newsroom in the old building was about 3,500 daily, and to the six Branch Reading Rooms about 2,300 daily. The former figure will probably be greatly increased with the improved accommodation now provided.

It is not an easy thing to foresee what the future of the Libraries in Cardiff will be. The great lesson of the early history of the Institution is a warning against attempting too much. There is equal if not greater danger in a policy of stagnation, but in Cardiff I think the pace is inclined to be too fast, and that what we most require to learn is how to make haste slowly. A great library can only be built up with years of patient and consistent work. We have the basis for a collection of books which may be of inestimable service to the community if proper attention is given to development on the right lines. And while not neglecting this aspect of the Library, it will also be possible to provide adequately for the wants of the outlying districts if the Corporation will only continue to deal generously by the Library.

THE MEN WHO HAVE TOILED.

It would be difficult to write an adequate account of all the men who in the past worked hard and patiently to sow the seed which has brought forth a goodly harvest for the town in the three institutions now so flourishing. Two names stand out prominently in the early history—Peter Price and Charles Thompson. The former toiled almost to the hour of his death for the Institution which he had virtually founded, and which he loved as one loves a favourite child. Mr. Thompson retired earlier, but he has given a host of gallant workers, not only to the Library and Museum, but to every good cause in Cardiff, in the persons of his sons. One serves on the Libraries Committee, another on the Museum Committee, and a third is Chairman of the Penarth Public Library Committee. I propose to give a brief account of these two pioneers of the Library.

PETER PRICE was born in the little country town of Builth, in Brecknockshire, in 1824, and was the youngest of a family of ten ; left fatherless at the age of seven, to be brought up by a widowed mother on straitened means, his regular education was limited to a few years at the school kept by the parson of the parish. He displayed marvellous aptitude for the acquirement of knowledge, and set about educating himself, and he continued his education up to the very last year of his life.

The Mechanics' Institute at Worcester first gave Mr. Price systematic help in his self-education. He was engaged in that town in the drawing office of an engineering firm.

In 1851 he came to Cardiff, and set up in business as a contractor, in partnership with his brother-in-law, and in a few years he was busily engaged advocating the adoption of the Public Libraries Act for the town. After the adoption of the Act he acted as hon. secretary for thirteen years. When he relinquished this office he still continued a member of the Committee, and was ultimately made vice-chairman, and during the last three years of his life he was chairman. He died October 4th, 1892. For thirty years he had watched the growth of the Institution, and he saw it develope from a thing of nothing to almost what it is to-day. This was his life-work, and will ever remain his most enduring memorial.

On the occasion of the opening of the then new building in 1882 a portrait of Mr. Price was painted by Mr. B. S. Marks, R.C.A., and presented by him to the Libraries Committee. This portrait will in future hang on the wall of the main staircase leading to the Reference Library. He took a keen interest in all that related to the education and welfare of the people. He was a member of the School Board for the first five years of its existence, a member of the Corporation for some years prior to his death; as Borough Magistrate, Governor of the University College, member of the Technical Instruction Committee, Governor of Wells' Charity, and in numerous other offices he served his town ungrudgingly and well.

The greatest act of his life, however, was one which I fear brought that life prematurely to a close. "In no public service did he set his fellow citizens a nobler example than in the splendid act of self-sacrifice in which the unspotted integrity of a life-time found final expression—the devotion, namely, of the whole of his savings to save the honour of the Building Society of which he was secretary." The loss of money was nothing to him in comparison with the respect and honour of his fellow men, which he retained, but the fact that his confidence had been betrayed by a servant whom he trusted and held in the greatest esteem was a blow from which he never recovered. It has been worthily said of him that he was—"Noble and generous in all he did, transparently sincere in all his actions, a serious and reverent student of nature, ever eager after knowledge, he kept, even to the end, the child-like in the larger mind."

CHARLES THOMPSON was born at Bridgwater in 1815. In 1842 he married MARIAN, the only daughter of Captain George Browne, R.N. (who was a Lieutenant on board the Victory at Trafalgar). In 1854 he entered into partnership with his brother-in-law, the late S. W. Browne, and with the late Wm. Allen in the corn and milling business of " Spiller & Browne."

The exigencies of the business caused his removal in 1857 to Cardiff, where a large steam mill had been erected, the precursor of the mills belonging to what is now the Limited Company, " Spillers & Bakers, Limited."

He took a house situated on the Newport Road, in the then newly erected " Halswell Terrace," where he lived till 1869, when he removed to his late residence Preswylfa, which he occupied till his death, which took place after a short illness on June 1st, 1889.

He was one of those who took an active part in the movement for the adoption of the Free Libraries Act in Cardiff, advocating it very strongly at the preliminary meeting, and also at the ratepayers' meeting in 1860, when the adoption of the Act was negatived.

He was also one of the small number who then subscribed to establish a Free Library on a voluntary basis. At the ratepayers' meeting in 1862 the motion for adopting the Act was proposed by Mr. Thompson and seconded by the late Dr. Vachell, and carried.

In all these proceedings he was very closely associated with the late Mr. Peter Price.

He was the first chairman, as Mr. Peter Price was the first hon. sec., of the Free Libraries Committee when formally constituted under the Act. He held that post for about ten years.

An interesting volume might be written of all the devoted workers who have passed away during the thirty-three years of the Library's existence. I should like to see portraits of some of these in stained glass fixed in the windows of the Library buildings. The men who quietly rendered yeoman service without reward and almost without recognition. Their names are many—it would be invidious to select from amongst them.

And it is satisfactory to record that many of those who toiled in the past are still with us honoured and respected, though they have ceased to render active service.

Never, perhaps, since the Institution began have so many able men been enlisted in its service as at the present time. The remarkable progress made in recent years is the best acknowledgment that can be made of their services. I hope we may long have the help of these and such as they.

THE PHILLIPPS COLLECTION OF WELSH MSS.

Since the foregoing pages were printed, a very important addition has been made to the Welsh Collections in the Library by the purchase of the Welsh portion of the Manuscripts collected by the late Sir Thomas Phillipps, Bart., F.R.S., of Middle Hill, Worcestershire, and Thirlestaine House, Cheltenham. This Prince of Book Collectors took special interest in the history and literature of Wales. He claimed descent from an ancient Pembrokeshire family, and partly on this account, and partly because of the wide range of his tastes, he acquired a large number of important Manuscripts relating to the Principality. Not only did he diligently search for such Manuscripts throughout the length and breadth of the country, but he also bought up entire collections such as those of Fenton, the Historian of Pembrokeshire, and the Rev. Thomas Price, of Cwmdû, better known as "Carnhuanawc."

The Collection includes one of the "Four Ancient Books of Wales," the famous "Book of Aneurin," written on vellum in the 12th century. This famous manuscript contains the Welsh epic poem called "The Gododin," which is supposed to have been composed in the 6th century. The next oldest manuscript in the Collection is a copy, on vellum, of the Dimetian Code of the Laws of Hywel Dha, ascribed to the 13th century, and believed to be the oldest MS. of this code in existence. There are several manuscripts in the handwriting of the eminent Welsh Antiquary, George Owen, of Henllys, including the original manuscript of "The Taylor's Cussion," a valuable collection of materials for Welsh history, the title of which is explained by a quaint verse on the title page—

> " The Taylor's Cussion made of shreedes
> Of divers peeces hath a patch
> So he that all this volume reedes
> Of divers thinges shall finde a snatch
> Therefore this booke of others all
> The Taylor's Cussion do I call."

There are valuable volumes of Welsh poetry, heraldic collections, deeds, charters, court and manor rolls, original letters, water-colour drawings, and original documents of various kinds.

The Collection was secured mainly through the public spirit of Mr. John Cory, Councillors Brain, Thomas, and Robinson, Mr. Marcus Gunn, and Mr. H. M. Thompson, who have given a Guarantee to the Bank for the amount of the purchase money.

The total cost of this valuable Collection was £3,666, towards which sum The Most Honourable The Marquess of Bute, K.T. gave £1,000, and Mr. John Cory, D.L., J.P., £500. Handsome contributions to the fund have also been given by The Right Honourable Lord Windsor (Mayor of Cardiff, 1895-6), The Right Honourable Lord Tredegar, Sir John Williams, Bart., M.D., The Mackintosh of Mackintosh and Mrs. Mackintosh, Mr. Henry Owen, F.S.A., Mr. D. C. Thomas, Mr. W. Llewellyn, D.L., J.P., The Rev. F. W. Edmondes, M.A., Colonel Bradney, Mr. J. Rogers Rees, Messrs. Sotheran & Co., and Mr. T. Mansel Franklen.